THE SONGS OF ANDREW LLOYD WEBBER™
40 OF HIS GREATEST

ANDREW LLOYD WEBBER™

Andrew Lloyd Webber™ is a trademark owned by Andrew Lloyd Webber.

ISBN 978-1-4768-1406-3

HAL•LEONARD®

7777 W. BLUEMOUND RD. P.O. BOX 13819 MILWAUKEE, WI 53213

In Australia Contact:
Hal Leonard Australia Pty. Ltd.
4 Lentara Court
Cheltenham, Victoria, 3192 Australia
Email: ausadmin@halleonard.com.au

Visit Hal Leonard Online at
www.halleonard.com

CONTENTS

4   All I Ask of You
FROM *THE PHANTOM OF THE OPERA*

6   Amigos Para Siempre
(Friends for Life)
THEME OF THE BARCELONA 1992 GAMES

8   Angel of Music
FROM *THE PHANTOM OF THE OPERA*

5   Another Suitcase in Another Hall
FROM *EVITA*

10   Any Dream Will Do
FROM *JOSEPH AND THE AMAZING
TECHNICOLOR® DREAMCOAT*

11   As If We Never Said Goodbye
FROM *SUNSET BOULEVARD*

12   Close Every Door
FROM *JOSEPH AND THE AMAZING
TECHNICOLOR® DREAMCOAT*

13   Don't Cry for Me Argentina
FROM *EVITA*

14   Everything's Alright
FROM *JESUS CHRIST SUPERSTAR*

16   High Flying, Adored
FROM *EVITA*

18   I Am the Starlight
FROM *STARLIGHT EXPRESS*

20   I Believe My Heart
FROM *THE WOMAN IN WHITE*

15   I Don't Know How to Love Him
FROM *JESUS CHRIST SUPERSTAR*

22   I'm Hopeless When
It Comes to You
FROM *STEPHEN WARD*

23   Learn to Be Lonely
FROM *THE PHANTOM OF THE OPERA*

24   Light at the End of the Tunnel
FROM *STARLIGHT EXPRESS*

26   Love Changes Everything
FROM *ASPECTS OF LOVE*

28   Love Never Dies
FROM *LOVE NEVER DIES*

30   Make Up My Heart
FROM *STARLIGHT EXPRESS*

27   Memory
FROM *CATS*

32 Mr. Mistoffelees
FROM *CATS*

34 The Music of the Night
FROM *THE PHANTOM OF THE OPERA*

35 No Matter What
FROM *WHISTLE DOWN THE WIND*

36 The Perfect Year
FROM *SUNSET BOULEVARD*

37 The Phantom of the Opera
FROM *THE PHANTOM OF THE OPERA*

38 Pie Jesu
FROM *REQUIEM*

40 The Point of No Return
FROM *THE PHANTOM OF THE OPERA*

42 Seeing Is Believing
FROM *ASPECTS OF LOVE*

39 Starlight Express
FROM *STARLIGHT EXPRESS*

44 Stick It to the Man
FROM *SCHOOL OF ROCK*

46 Superstar
FROM *JESUS CHRIST SUPERSTAR*

48 Take That Look Off Your Face
FROM *SONG & DANCE*

47 Tell Me on a Sunday
FROM *SONG & DANCE*

50 Think of Me
FROM *THE PHANTOM OF THE OPERA*

51 'Til I Hear You Sing
FROM *LOVE NEVER DIES*

52 Unexpected Song
FROM *SONG & DANCE*

53 Whistle Down the Wind
FROM *WHISTLE DOWN THE WIND*

54 Wishing You Were
Somehow Here Again
FROM *THE PHANTOM OF THE OPERA*

55 With One Look
FROM *SUNSET BOULEVARD*

56 You Must Love Me
FROM *EVITA*

ALL I ASK OF YOU

from THE PHANTOM OF THE OPERA

VIOLA

Music by ANDREW LLOYD WEBBER
Lyrics by CHARLES HART
Additional Lyrics by RICHARD STILGOE

Moderately slow

ANOTHER SUITCASE IN ANOTHER HALL

from EVITA

VIOLA

Words by TIM RICE
Music by ANDREW LLOYD WEBBER

AMIGOS PARA SIEMPRE
(Friends for Life)
(The Official Theme of the Barcelona 1992 Games)

VIOLA

Music by ANDREW LLOYD WEBBER
Lyrics by DON BLACK

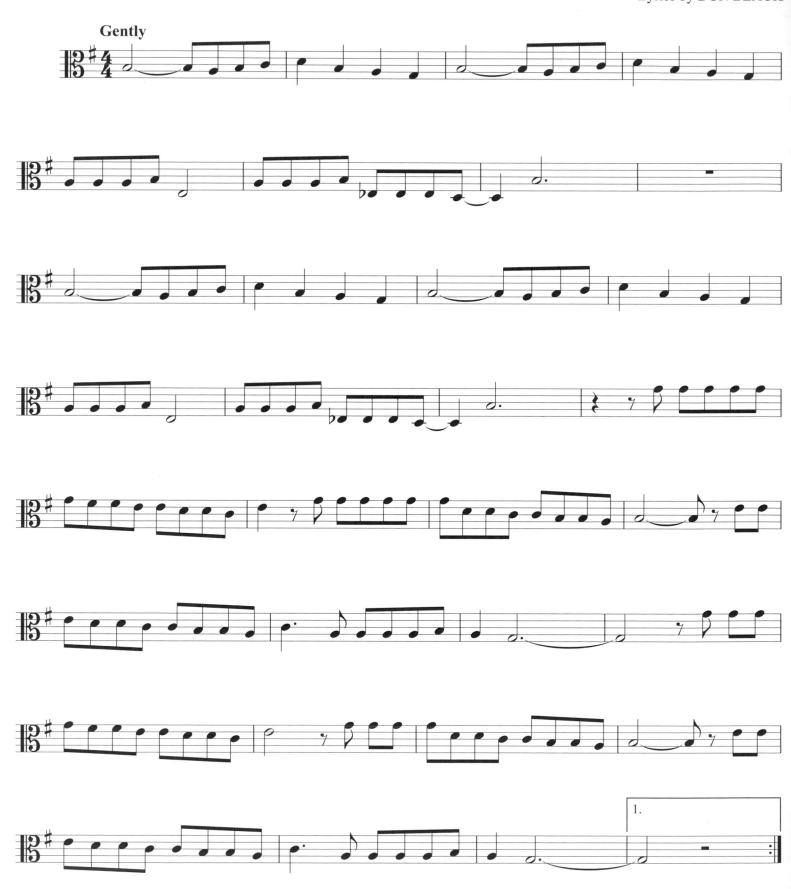

ANGEL OF MUSIC
from THE PHANTOM OF THE OPERA

VIOLA

Music by ANDREW LLOYD WEBBER
Lyrics by CHARLES HART
Additional Lyrics by RICHARD STILGOE

ANY DREAM WILL DO
from JOSEPH AND THE AMAZING TECHNICOLOR® DREAMCOAT

VIOLA

Music by ANDREW LLOYD WEBBER
Lyrics by TIM RICE

AS IF WE NEVER SAID GOODBYE

from SUNSET BOULEVARD

VIOLA

Music by ANDREW LLOYD WEBBER
Lyrics by DON BLACK and CHRISTOPHER HAMPTON,
with contributions by AMY POWERS

CLOSE EVERY DOOR
from JOSEPH AND THE AMAZING TECHNICOLOR® DREAMCOAT

VIOLA

Music by ANDREW LLOYD WEBBER
Lyrics by TIM RICE

Moderately, expressively

DON'T CRY FOR ME ARGENTINA
from EVITA

VIOLA

Words by TIM RICE
Music by ANDREW LLOYD WEBBER

EVERYTHING'S ALRIGHT
from JESUS CHRIST SUPERSTAR

VIOLA

Words by TIM RICE
Music by ANDREW LLOYD WEBBER

I DON'T KNOW HOW TO LOVE HIM

from JESUS CHRIST SUPERSTAR

VIOLA

Words by TIM RICE
Music by ANDREW LLOYD WEBBER

HIGH FLYING, ADORED

from EVITA

VIOLA

Words by TIM RICE
Music by ANDREW LLOYD WEBBER

Moderately

I AM THE STARLIGHT

from STARLIGHT EXPRESS

VIOLA

Music by ANDREW LLOYD WEBBER
Lyrics by RICHARD STILGOE

Moderately

I BELIEVE MY HEART

from THE WOMAN IN WHITE

VIOLA

Music by ANDREW LLOYD WEBBER
Lyrics by DAVID ZIPPEL

I'M HOPELESS WHEN IT COMES TO YOU

from STEPHEN WARD

VIOLA

Music by ANDREW LLOYD WEBBER
Book and Lyrics by DON BLACK
and CHRISTOPHER HAMPTON

LEARN TO BE LONELY
from THE PHANTOM OF THE OPERA

VIOLA

Music by ANDREW LLOYD WEBBER
Lyrics by CHARLES HART

LIGHT AT THE END OF THE TUNNEL

from STARLIGHT EXPRESS

VIOLA

Music by ANDREW LLOYD WEBBER
Lyrics by RICHARD STILGOE

25

LOVE CHANGES EVERYTHING

from ASPECTS OF LOVE

VIOLA

Music by ANDREW LLOYD WEBBER
Lyrics by DON BLACK and CHARLES HART

MEMORY
from CATS

VIOLA

Music by ANDREW LLOYD WEBBER
Text by TREVOR NUNN after T.S. ELIOT

LOVE NEVER DIES

from LOVE NEVER DIES

VIOLA

Music by ANDREW LLOYD WEBBER
Lyrics by GLENN SLATER

MAKE UP MY HEART
from STARLIGHT EXPRESS

VIOLA

Music by ANDREW LLOYD WEBBER
Lyrics by RICHARD STILGOE

Moderately

MR. MISTOFFELEES
from CATS

VIOLA

Music by ANDREW LLOYD WEBBER
Text by T.S. ELIOT

THE MUSIC OF THE NIGHT
from THE PHANTOM OF THE OPERA

VIOLA

Music by ANDREW LLOYD WEBBER
Lyrics by CHARLES HART
Additional Lyrics by RICHARD STILGOE

NO MATTER WHAT

from WHISTLE DOWN THE WIND

Music by ANDREW LLOYD WEBBER
Lyrics by JIM STEINMAN

VIOLA

THE PERFECT YEAR
from SUNSET BOULEVARD

VIOLA

Music by ANDREW LLOYD WEBBER
Lyrics by DON BLACK
and CHRISTOPHER HAMPTON

THE PHANTOM OF THE OPERA
from THE PHANTOM OF THE OPERA

VIOLA

Music by ANDREW LLOYD WEBBER
Lyrics by CHARLES HART
Additional Lyrics by RICHARD STILGOE
and MIKE BATT

PIE JESU
from REQUIEM

VIOLA

By ANDREW LLOYD WEBBER

STARLIGHT EXPRESS
from STARLIGHT EXPRESS

VIOLA

Music by ANDREW LLOYD WEBBER
Lyrics by RICHARD STILGOE

THE POINT OF NO RETURN
from THE PHANTOM OF THE OPERA

VIOLA

Music by ANDREW LLOYD WEBBER
Lyrics by CHARLES HART
Additional Lyrics by RICHARD STILGOE

SEEING IS BELIEVING

from ASPECTS OF LOVE

VIOLA

Music by ANDREW LLOYD WEBBER
Lyrics by DON BLACK and CHARLES HART

STICK IT TO THE MAN

from SCHOOL OF ROCK

VIOLA

Music by ANDREW LLOYD WEBBER
Lyrics by GLENN SLATER

(small notes optional)

SUPERSTAR
from JESUS CHRIST SUPERSTAR

VIOLA

Words by TIM RICE
Music by ANDREW LLOYD WEBBER

TELL ME ON A SUNDAY

from SONG & DANCE

Music by ANDREW LLOYD WEBBER
Lyrics by DON BLACK

VIOLA

TAKE THAT LOOK OFF YOUR FACE
from SONG & DANCE

VIOLA

Music by ANDREW LLOYD WEBBER
Lyrics by DON BLACK

THINK OF ME
from THE PHANTOM OF THE OPERA

VIOLA

Music by ANDREW LLOYD WEBBER
Lyrics by CHARLES HART
Additional Lyrics by RICHARD STILGOE

'TIL I HEAR YOU SING

from LOVE NEVER DIES

VIOLA

Music by ANDREW LLOYD WEBBER
Lyrics by GLENN SLATER

UNEXPECTED SONG
from SONG & DANCE

VIOLA

Music by ANDREW LLOYD WEBBER
Lyrics by DON BLACK

WHISTLE DOWN THE WIND
from WHISTLE DOWN THE WIND

VIOLA

Music by ANDREW LLOYD WEBBER
Lyrics by JIM STEINMAN

WISHING YOU WERE SOMEHOW HERE AGAIN

from THE PHANTOM OF THE OPERA

VIOLA

Music by ANDREW LLOYD WEBBER
Lyrics by CHARLES HART
Additional Lyrics by RICHARD STILGOE

WITH ONE LOOK

from SUNSET BOULEVARD

VIOLA

Music by ANDREW LLOYD WEBBER
Lyrics by DON BLACK and CHRISTOPHER HAMPTON,
with contributions by AMY POWERS

YOU MUST LOVE ME
from the Cinergi Motion Picture EVITA

VIOLA

Words by TIM RICE
Music by ANDREW LLOYD WEBBER